Handmade Christmas Crafts

Publications International, Ltd.

The Herald Angel Pin on pages 22–23 is courtesy of
The Beadery Craft Products.

Louis Weber, CEO
Publications International, Ltd.
7373 North Cicero Avenue
Lincolnwood, Illinois 60712

Manufactured in China.

8 7 6 5 4 3 2 1

ISBN: 1-4127-1058-8

Contents

Tips and Techniques

Christmas can be the warmest and happiest season of the year for many people—even though time always seems at a premium. The holidays are also when creating decorations and presents is most fun and fulfilling—and appreciated by those receiving the lovingly made gifts. With *Handmade Christmas Crafts,* you'll find many projects that take a day or less to create. These are things made by hand that come from the heart.

The projects in this book include a variety of techniques and methods. Crafting is a wonderful way to escape crowded shopping malls and the mad race to find that "perfect" gift. Teach your kids how wonderful homemade crafts are by helping them create some of the included projects. (Be sure to assist them while they are crafting; some of the projects require the use of potentially dangerous tools, such as glue guns!) Best of all, each project has complete step-by-step instructions and photos to help make everything easy to understand and fun to do.

General Pattern Instructions

When a project's instructions tell you to cut out a shape according to the pattern, trace the pattern from the book onto tracing paper, using a pencil. If the pattern has a dotted line, it is a half pattern. Fold a sheet of tracing paper in half, and open up the paper. Place the fold line of the tracing paper exactly on top of the dotted line of the pattern, and trace the pattern with a pencil. Then refold and cut along the line, going through both layers. Open the paper for the full pattern.

Some of the patterns in this book are printed smaller than actual size in order to fit on the page. You will have to enlarge them on a photocopier before using them, copying the pattern at the percentage indicated near the pattern.

Transferring Designs

You don't have to know anything about drawing to transfer a design. The designs in this book can be transferred directly onto the project surface.

Transfer supplies: tracing paper, tape, pencil or fine marker, transfer paper (carbon or graphite), and stylus

1 Place transparent tracing paper over the design you want to copy. Tape a few edges down to hold the pattern in place. Trace the design lines with a pencil or fine marker. Trace only the lines you absolutely need to complete the project.

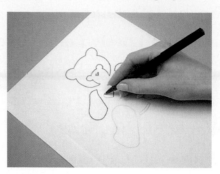

2 Place a piece of transfer paper, carbon side down, between the surface and the pattern. Choose a color of paper that will easily show on your project, and use a stylus or pencil to trace over the design lines. Lift a corner of the pattern to make sure the design is transferring properly.

Sewing

Before plunging into a sewing project, check to make sure you have all the materials needed. Most of the items you need will probably be on hand already:

Fabrics: The type of fabric best suited to the project is given in the list of materials. But don't hesitate to make substitutions, taking into consideration your preferences in colors and patterns. Keep in mind the scale of a pattern relative to the size of the project. The weight of the fabric is an important consideration: Don't substitute a heavy, stiff fabric for a delicate one.

Scissors: Two styles are needed, one about 8 to 10 inches long with a bent handle for cutting fabric. This style of scissors enables you to cut through the fabric while the fabric lays flat. These shears should be sharp and used only for fabric. The second style of scissors is smaller, about 6 inches, with sharp points. You will need this style for smaller projects and close areas.

Straight pins: Nonrusting dressmaker pins are best to use because they will not leave rust marks on your fabric if they come in contact with dampness or glue. They also have very sharp points for easy insertion.

Tape measure: This should be plastic coated so it won't stretch and can be wiped off if it comes in contact with paint or glue.

Ironing board and steam iron: Be sure your ironing board is padded and has a clean covering. Sometimes you do more sewing with the iron than you do with the sewing machine. Keeping your fabrics, seams, and hems pressed cuts down on stitches and valuable time. It is important to press your fabric to achieve a professional look. The iron is also used to adhere fusible interfacing. Keep the bottom of your iron clean and free of any substance that could mark your fabric. The steam iron may be used directly on most fabrics with no shine. Test a small piece of the fabric first. If it causes a shine on the right side, iron on the reverse side.

Thread: Have mercerized sewing thread in the colors needed for each project you have chosen. Proper shade and strength (about 50 weight) of thread avoids having the stitching show more than is necessary and will give the item a more finished look.

Fusible webbing (or adhesive): A lightweight fusible iron-on adhesive is time-saving and easy to use. The webbing is placed paper side up on the wrong side of the material. Place iron on paper side of adhesive, and press for 1 to 3 seconds. Allow fabric to cool. The design can then be drawn or traced onto the paper side and cut out. Remove the paper, place the material right side up in the desired position on the project, and iron for 3 to 5 seconds.

Sewing machine: Neat, even stitches are achieved in very few minutes with a sewing machine. If desired, you may machine-stitch a zigzag stitch around the attached fusible adhesive pieces to secure the edges.

Work surface: Your sewing surface should be a comfortable height for sitting and roomy enough to lay out your projects. Keep it clean and free of other crafting materials that could accidentally spill and soil your fabric.

Mitering Corners

1 Find the center of each border strip and the center of each side of the quilt. One side at a time, pin the border and stitch, beginning and ending ¼ inch from the edge of the quilt top. (Borders need strips longer than the sides for mitering.)

2 With right sides together, fold the quilt top diagonally, matching seams and the edges of the borders. Use a ruler and pencil to extend across the border strips to the line formed by the fold.

3 Taking care not to snag the seam allowances, stitch from the inside edge of the border to the outer corner on the marked line. Trim the ends of the border strips, and press the seam open. Repeat for each corner.

Knitting

The knitted projects featured in this book require basic knitting knowledge and tools, many of which you may already have on hand:

Needles: Pairs of knitting needles are available in aluminum, plastic, and bamboo, in varying lengths. Needles should be straight and have nicely rounded points; blunt, bent, or scratched needles will decrease the speed and efficiency of your knitting. Some projects will require double-pointed needles, which are available in traditional sizes and come in sets of either four or five. They are mainly used to create seamless garments.

Stitch gauge: This is used to count stitches on a gauge sample to check tension of the yarn.

Stitch markers: Available in different colors and sizes, stitch markers make it easier to count stitches and rows.

Stitch holders: These look like long safety pins and are designed to hold stitches that have been slipped off the needle to be worked later.

Crochet hooks: They come in handy for picking up dropped stitches.

Tapestry needle: This needle has a large eye and blunt point that slips easily between stitches. Do not use a sharp pointed needle, as it may split the yarn.

Each knitting project also includes the size of the finished knitted item, when possible, as well as the recommended yarn. The instructions will suggest how many balls or skeins are needed for the size indicated, how much each ball/skein weighs, and its yardage.

Be sure to check your gauge before embarking on any knitting project. If the needles indicated with the project do not produce the gauge listed, use a different size until you achieve the proper gauge.

Felting

Some of the projects in this book are knitted and then felted, creating a dense, shrunken fabric. To felt a knitted item, set your washing machine on the hot water cycle and low water level. Add a small amount of dishwashing liquid (too many suds will hamper the felting process). Turn on the machine, and let it agitate for 5 minutes. Stop the machine, and check to determine the amount of felting (the time will vary depending on the yarn, washing machine, and hardness of water). Continue to check every 5 minutes until the stitches completely disappear and the felted item is the desired size. You can add towels, tennis balls, or washable sneakers to the machine to help balance the load and aid the process.

Once desired felting is obtained, remove the item from the machine, drain the soapy water, and fill the machine with cold rinse water. Soak the item in rinse water for several minutes to remove all soap. Set the machine on the spin cycle to eliminate excess water from the felted item, or wrap the item in large towels and squeeze out the rinse water. Remove felted item from the machine immediately after spinning to avoid wrinkling. Stretch, pull, and pat the item into desired shape, and let dry on a flat surface.

Basic Knitting Stitches and Abbreviations

Following are some basic knitting stitches and abbreviations used throughout the book:
beg: begin
BO: bind off
CO: cast on
cont: continue
k: knit

k2tog: knit 2 stitches together

m1: make 1 stitch (insert left needle from front to back under horizontal strand between stitch just worked and next stitch on left needle, then knit this strand through back loop)

p: purl

p2tog: purl 2 stitches together

pm: place marker

rem: remaining

rep: repeat

rnd: round

RS: round side

sl st: slip stitch, unworked, off of one needle to other needle

sl st knitwise: slip stitch knitwise by inserting needle as if you were going to knit stitch

sl st purlwise: slip stitch purlwise by inserting needle as if you were going to purl stitch

ssk: slip next 2 stitches knitwise, then insert tip of left needle into front of these 2 stitches and knit them together

st(s): stitch(es)

St st: stockinette stitch (knit on right side, purl on wrong side)

tog: together

WS: wrong side

[ ]: repeat instructions inside brackets as indicated

A Word About Glue

Glue can be a sticky subject when you don't use the right one for the job. There are many different glues on the craft market today, each formulated for a different crafting purpose. The following are ones you should be familiar with:

White glue: This may be used as an all-purpose glue. It dries clear and flexible. It is often referred to as craft or tacky glue. Tacky on contact, it allows you to put 2 items together without a lot of setup time required. Use it for most projects, especially ones involving wood, plastics, some fabrics, and cardboard.

Fabric glue: This type of glue is made to bond with fabric fibers and to withstand repeated washing. Use this glue for attaching decorations to fabric projects. Some glues require heat-setting. Check the bottle for complete instructions.

Hot glue: Formed into cylindrical sticks, this glue is inserted into a hot-temperature glue gun and heated to liquid state. Depending on the type of glue gun used, the glue is forced out through the gun's nozzle by either pushing on the end of the glue stick or squeezing a trigger.

Use clear glue sticks for projects using wood, fabrics, most plastics, ceramics, and cardboard. When using any glue gun, be careful of the nozzle and the freshly applied glue—they are very hot! Apply glue to the piece being attached. Work with small areas at a time so that the glue doesn't set before being pressed into place.

Low-temperature glue: This is similar to hot glue in that it is formed into sticks and requires a glue gun to be used. Low-temperature glue is used for projects that would be damaged by heat, such as foam, balloons, and metallic ribbons.

Decorative Painting

There are a wide variety of paint brands. Acrylic paints are available at your local arts and crafts stores. This type of paint dries in minutes and allows projects to be completed fairly quickly. Clean hands and brushes with soap and water.

Some projects may require a medium that is not acrylic or waterbase. These require mineral spirits to clean up. Always check the manufacturer's label before working with a product so you can have the proper cleaning supplies on hand.

Varnishes

Choose from a wide variety of varnishes to protect your finished project. Varnish is available in both spray or brush on. Brush-on waterbase varnishes dry in minutes and clean up with soap and water. Use over any acrylic paint. Don't use over paints or mediums requiring mineral spirits to clean up. Spray varnishes can be used over any type of paint or medium. Varnishes are available in matte, satin, or gloss finishes. Choose the finish you prefer.

Brushes

Foam (sponge) brushes: These work well to seal, basecoat, and varnish surfaces. Clean foam brushes with soap and water when using acrylic paints and mediums. For paints or mediums that require mineral spirits to clean up, you will have to throw away the disposable brush.

Synthetic brushes: Use with acrylic paints for details and designs. You will use a liner brush for thin lines and details. A script brush is needed for extra long lines. Round brushes are used to fill in round areas, for stroke work, and to make broad lines. An angle brush is used to fill in large areas, float, or side load color. A large flat brush is used to apply basecoat and varnish. Small flat brushes are for stroke work and basecoating small areas.

Basic Painting Techniques

Thin Lines

1 Thin paint with 50 percent water for a fluid consistency that flows easily off the brush (about ink consistency).

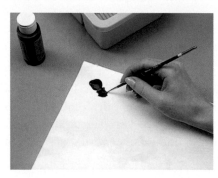

2 Use a liner brush for short lines and tiny details or a script brush for long lines. Dip brush into thinned paint. Wipe excess on palette.

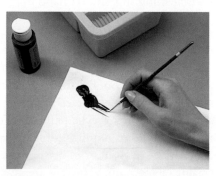

3 Hold brush upright with handle pointing to the ceiling. Use your little finger as a balance when painting. Don't apply pressure for extra thin lines.

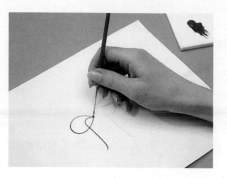

Spattering

The spatter-paint technique is used to create little dots of paint sprinkled on a surface—great for creating snow, aged flyspeck look, or just adding fun colors to a finish. Always test spattering on scrap paper first.

1 Thin paint with 50 to 80 percent water. Use an old toothbrush and a palette knife, or use a Kemper tool. Dip brush into thinned paint. Lots of paint on the brush will create large dots. As paint runs out, dots become finer.

2 Drag your thumb or palette knife across the top of the bristles, causing them to bend. As they are released, the bristles spring forward, spattering the paint onto the surface.

Dots

Perfectly round dots can be made with any round implement. The size of the implement determines the size of the dot. You can use the wooden end of a paintbrush, a stylus tip, a pencil tip, or the eraser end of a pencil (with an unused eraser).

Use undiluted paint for thick dots, or dilute paint with 50 percent water for smooth dots. Dip the tip into paint and then onto the surface. For uniform dots, you must redip in the paint for each dot. For graduated dots, continue dotting with the same paint load. Clean tip on paper towel after each group, and reload.

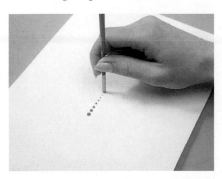

Making a Bow

There are many ways to make bows, and the more you make, the easier it becomes. Cutting the ends of a ribbon at an angle lends a more polished appearance to the finished product.

Multiloop Bow

1 Unroll several yards from a bolt of ribbon. Form loops from ribbon with your dominant hand. Pinch center of loops with thumb and forefinger of your other hand as you work.

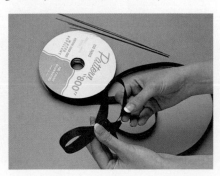

2 Continue to add loops to your bow. Keep pinching the bow's center with your thumb and forefinger. After you have all the loops you desire, trim away excess ribbon from the bolt. If you want a streamer, leave the ribbon longer before cutting.

3 Insert a length of wire around the center of the ribbon. Bring the 2 wire ends securely and tightly next to the bow's center to eliminate loop slippage. Attach the bow to your project with the wire. You can also trim the wire and glue the bow in place.

Note: When using heavier ribbon, use a chenille stem to secure the bow. The tiny hairs on the stem will hold the bow securely and not allow potential twisting of the bare wire. For tiny, delicate bows, thin cloth-covered wire can be used for securing. It eliminates slipping and is so tiny that it disappears into the bow loops.

Lush and Lovely
Lodge Wreath

*Beautifully textured evergreens, bright red berries, and a bold ribbon
will make this charming wreath a holiday favorite.*

what you'll need

20-inch artificial
evergreen wreath of
mixed greens

2 black chenille stems

1½ yards red-and-black
plaid ribbon, 2½ inches
wide

Hot glue gun and
glue sticks

10 pinecones

6 dried pomegranates

Heavy-duty scissors or
wire cutters

Ruler

Assorted foliage

Berry clusters:
4 burgundy and 4 red

2 red berry sprays,
12 inches each

tip
When working on a wreath or another floral arrangement that is designed to hang, you may want to work with it in a hanging position to get the right perspective.

4 Cut pomegranate stems to 1 inch, and glue 2 pomegranates in center of bow. Glue remaining pomegranates in clusters of 2, equally spaced around wreath.

5 Cut foliage into short lengths, and glue between cones and pomegranates. Glue a few sprigs over top of bow.

1 Shape wreath to increase fullness and achieve a natural look. To make hanger, twist a chenille stem into loop on top back of wreath.

2 About 12 inches from one end of ribbon, form two 6-inch loops. Pinch loops together, and secure with chenille stem to form bow. Note: If you can't find a ribbon you like, cut 3-inch-wide fabric strips, and turn and glue the edges under slightly. Then form a bow as you would with a ribbon.

3 Glue bow to upper left side of wreath. Weave bow's streamers into wreath, and glue in place. Glue cones in wreath as shown.

6 Glue burgundy berry clusters equally spaced around wreath; repeat with red berry clusters. Cut red berry sprays into 4-inch lengths, and glue into wreath as desired.

Sending
Holiday Wishes

Making holiday greeting cards to send to your loved ones tells them how much you really value them—often more than even your words can convey!

what you'll need

5¼×15¾-inch piece white paper

Ruler

Patterns on page 13

Pencil

Scissors

5¼×7¼-inch piece black paper

⅛-inch hole punch

White glue

2 pieces green paper, 7×5 inches each

Scrap yellow paper

1 Fold a short end of the white paper up to create a 1¼-inch flap. Fold remaining length of paper in half to form a card.

2 Trace snowbank pattern onto flap. Cut out snowbank shape.

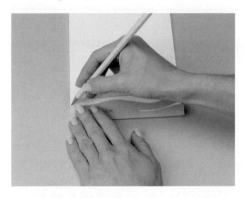

3 Punch 8 holes in black paper with hole punch, leaving middle of card for tree placement. Glue black paper to front of card.

4 Trace tree pattern onto each piece of green paper, and cut out. Fold each tree in half lengthwise.

5 Glue a tree to middle of card, above snowbank flap. Glue fold of other tree on fold line of glued-down tree.

6 Cut star from yellow paper, and glue at top of tree.

try this!

Try this snowflake variation. Draw a snowflake pattern on a household sponge, and cut it out. Sponge-paint snowflakes onto pieces of white paper. When paint is dry, place vellum on top of snowflakes, and use ribbon to attach the pieces of paper. Use a silver pen to write a special greeting.

patterns

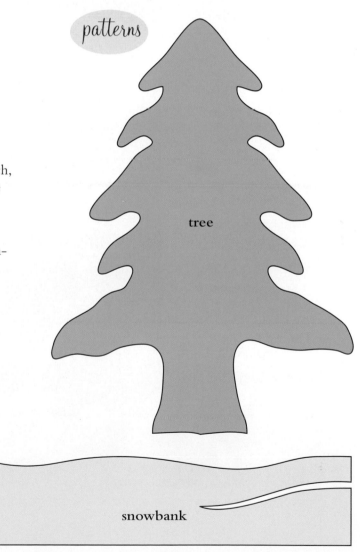

tree

snowbank

Lost Mitten Tree
Folk-Art Pillow

This folk-art pillow is sure to be one of your family's favorites from year to year. And what a great gift to warm a friend's living room. Try crafting your own design for yet another festive holiday touch!

what you'll need

Felt: 3 shades of green, 6×9 inches each; gold, 5-inch square; and scraps of red, orange, purple, pink, and turquoise, about 2×3 inches each

Iron-on adhesive

Scissors

Iron and ironing board

Patterns on page 15

White paper

Pencil

2 square red fringed napkins, 18 inches each

Washable glue (optional)

Toothpicks (optional)

Straight pins

Sewing machine

Thread to match napkins

8-ounce bag fiberfill

1 Cut pieces of iron-on adhesive to match sizes of felt pieces, and following manufacturer's directions, adhere to felt.

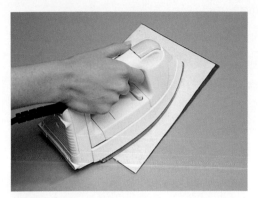

2 Trace mitten and star patterns below onto white paper; cut out. On paper backing of 1 shade of green felt, trace around mitten 4 times. Turn pattern over, and trace 4 more times. On 2 other shades of green felt, trace mitten 3 times in each direction. (You will have a total of 20 mittens.) Trace star on paper backing of gold felt.

3 From gold and remaining colors of felt, cut out small circles, hearts, stars, V shapes, squares, zigzag lines, straight lines, and wavy lines. These will be used to decorate the mittens.

4 Arrange undecorated mittens on napkin in a pyramid shape with 6 mittens on the bottom (leave room at top for star). Each row should have 1 less mitten than the row below it. Make a chart of how you have your mittens arranged. Remove all but bottom row of mittens from napkin.

patterns

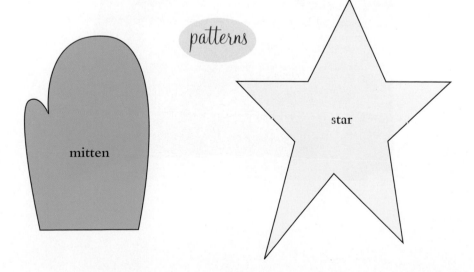

mitten

star

5 Select some colorful felt shapes to embellish your bottom row of mittens. Trim them to fit mittens. Remove paper backing from embellishments and mittens. Following manufacturer's directions, fuse embellishments and mittens to napkin. (Fusing may take several seconds longer than suggested, due to thickness of felt.)

6 Referring to your chart, reposition next row of 5 mittens, removing paper backings and embellishing them as you go. Fuse to napkin. Repeat for each row of mittens. Adhere gold star to top of mitten tree. Note: If some felt pieces have not adhered well, use a toothpick to spread washable glue underneath sides.

7 Matching up edges, pin 2 napkins with wrong sides together. Sew about ⅛ inch inside fringe around pillow, leaving about 8 inches open on bottom.

8 Stuff pillow with entire bag of fiberfill. Sew bottom opening closed. Spot clean when necessary.

Simply
Elegant Scarf

Warm up a loved one's holiday with this luxurious but easy-to-make scarf. Knitted in simple garter stitch, it can be completed in just a couple of evenings, even by a novice knitter. Make an assortment so you can check off several gifts on your Christmas list!

what you'll need

160 yards mohair blend yarn

160 yards sparkling heavy thread or thin yarn

U.S. size 11 knitting needles

Tape measure

Scissors

Tapestry needle

See pages 6–7 for knitting tips and abbreviations.

Gauge: 12 sts=4 inches in garter st (exact gauge not important; scarf can be slightly wider or narrower)

1 Holding both yarns tog, CO 20 sts.

2 Use garter st (k every row) until work measures about 55 inches in length.

3 BO all sts. Cut off excess yarn, leaving a tail. Thread tail on tapestry needle, and weave into final row of sts for 2 or 3 inches.

try this!

You'll be amazed at how many different looks you can achieve just by changing the yarn combinations you use for this scarf. Be creative!

Mini-Scene
Ornament

You've wondered about those ships in bottles.
Now there are snowpeople in teardrop globes—and they don't even
melt! Your kids are sure to think these are the coolest.

what you'll need

2½×5-inch plastic teardrop globe

White dimensional paint

Ruler

Poms: one 1½-inch white, two 1-inch white, and two ¼-inch red

Low-temperature glue gun and glue sticks

Chenille stem: 6-inch length white and 1½-inch length green

Felt: ¼×6-inch green, 1-square-inch pink, and ½×1-inch orange

Scissors

Patterns on page 19

Tracing paper

Pencil

Two 7mm wiggle eyes

Three 4mm red beads

Small amount fiberfill

⅛-inch-wide satin ribbon: 18 inches green and 26 inches red

⅝-inch jingle bells: one each red, green, and white

1 Separate the globe halves. Using the white dimensional paint, squeeze dots inside each half to give the effect of snow. Space the dots about ½ inch apart. It might be helpful to imagine triangles and place a dot at each point. Let the paint dry.

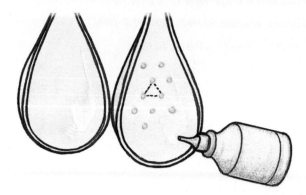

2 To assemble the snowperson, glue the 1½-inch pom (bottom) to a 1-inch pom (middle). Next, glue the other 1-inch pom (head) to top of the middle pom. For the arms, fold in 1½ inches on both ends of a 6-inch length chenille stem. Bend the folded stem into a C shape. Glue the inside of the C shape to the back of the figure.

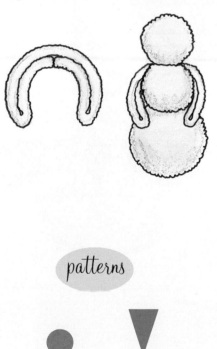

patterns

● cheek   ▼ nose

3 To make the scarf, angle-cut the green felt at both ends. Wrap the middle of the scarf around the neck, and tie on one side. Using the patterns below, trace and cut two pink felt cheeks and one orange felt nose. Glue the cheeks to the face just above the scarf. Glue the nose to the center of the face between the cheeks. Glue the eyes so that they touch the top inside area of the cheeks. For the earmuffs, bend the 1½-inch length of green chenille into a C shape, and glue it to the top of the head. Glue red poms over both ends of the green chenille. Glue three beads down the front.

4 Glue a small amount of fiberfill inside the back half of the globe for a snowbank. Glue the finished snowperson on top of the snow. Close the halves. For the bow, use the green ribbon and cut one 18-inch length of red ribbon. Thread two jingle bells onto one ribbon and one jingle bell onto the other. Keeping the bells on the ribbons, insert both ribbons through globe loop. Tie a bow using both ribbons. For a hanger, thread the remaining 8-inch length of red ribbon through the globe loop and knot the ends together.

Stained Glass
Sun Catchers

These elegant Christmas decorations will make even a novice crafter look like a professional in no time. Using foil tape as leading, small bits of glass really come to life!

what you'll need

Stained glass chips or ⅛-inch thick glass sheets

Safety goggles

Work gloves

Paper grocery bag

Hammer

Strainer

Paper towels

Roundnose jewelry pliers

Pencil and paper (optional)

Silver or gold foil tape

Scissors

Craft stick

Glass or metal adhesive

Clear marbles (optional)

18-gauge uncoated floral stem wire

Ruler

Wire cutters

Mini suction cups

Note: If using stained glass chips, start at step 2.

1 Wearing safety goggles and work gloves, place large sheets of glass into grocery bag, and lightly tap with hammer. Remove pieces, place in strainer, and rinse under running water to remove small particles of glass. Place glass pieces on paper towels to dry. Repeat for all colors. (Remove unwanted pointed ends or sharp edges with pliers.)

2 Use various glass pieces to create desired shape. You may want to trace pieces onto paper to help you re-create placement when you're ready to assemble. Wrap outer edges of each glass piece with foil tape, overlap ends slightly, and cut off any excess tape. Fold foil over top and bottom edges. Smooth all sides with craft stick.

3 Glue pieces together with glass or metal adhesive, layering them on top of one another. If you're making a poinsettia or an angel sun

catcher, adhere marbles as shown on opposite page. Let dry 8 hours.

4 Turn sun catcher over. Cut 1½-inch length of wire with wire cutters. Use roundnose jewelry pliers to curl ends, then bend at center to create looped hanger. Adhere to top of sun catcher with adhesive. For angel sun catcher, add decorative touch by cutting, curling, and adhering 3 pieces of wire to back of "skirt." Let dry at least 24 hours before hanging sun catchers on suction cups.

try this!

To create an ornamental S hook to use for hanging, cut a 3-inch piece of wire. Bend as shown on opposite page using jewelry pliers. Slip smallest end of S hook through hanger loop at top of sun catcher, then press small end of hook closed.

Herald
Angel Pin

This angel's so sweet and pretty, she's certain
to brighten a coat or a sweater. Change the stones or the beads
to reflect your own sparkling personality.

what you'll need

One 3×5-inch index card or similar card stock

Ruler

Scissors

White glue or low-temperature glue gun and glue sticks

One 25×18mm pear-shaped acrylic cabochon (antique white pearl)

Two 15×11mm pear-shaped acrylic cabochons (antique white pearl)

One 12mm round acrylic cabochon (antique white pearl)

One 10×8mm oval acrylic cabochon (antique white pearl)

15 inches of #50 gold braided cord

One 18mm round acrylic faceted stone (topaz)

Three 4×8mm navette acrylic faceted stones (emerald)

Three 5mm round acrylic cabochons (dark amethyst)

Two 4×6mm oval acrylic faceted stones (ruby)

One 25mm round acrylic mirror (topaz)

One 18mm round acrylic mirror (topaz)

One pin back

1 Cut two pieces from index card: one ⅛×1½ inches and the second ⅛×¾ inch. Glue them in a cross formation. Glue pearl cabochons on cross (see photo of finished pin).

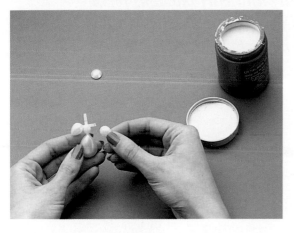

2 Starting under one wing, carefully glue gold cord around pearl cabochons in a figure-eight fashion. Hide ends of cord under crossover between two beads.

3 Glue 18mm topaz faceted stone under angel's head. Glue three emerald navettes, three dark amethyst cabochons, and two ruby oval faceted stones to edges of topaz mirrors. Glue mirrors to underside of angel. Glue pin back to back of entire piece.

Four
Calling Birds

Four snowy birds call out a message of goodwill to all.
Birch branches trimmed with holly and tiny blossoms form
a unique wreath. It looks like this frosty foursome has made a
charming wreath their new home for the holidays!

what you'll need

Stem floral wire,
22 gauge

Brown floral tape

Wire cutters

Birch branches, about
24 inches in length
(between 140 and
170 branches)

4 matching birds

Hot glue gun and
glue sticks

Spanish moss

2 stems silk holly

2 stems white silk
miniature roses

Miniature pinecones

White glue

Small artist's paintbrush

Diamond dust or
opalescent glitter

1 Wrap and cut floral wire with brown floral
tape. Separate branches into 4 bundles with
about 36 thin branch pieces in each and another
2 bundles with 10 to 15 branches each.

2 With taped wire, tie each bundle in middle, then tie on each end. Add extra branches as needed to make solid bundles.

3 Make a square with 4 large bundles, and wrap ends together with wire. Square should measure about 18×18 inches. Leave a few light branches longer at corners to soften wreath. Trim remaining branches so wreath has a flat back for hanging.

4 Wire 2 smaller bundles to back of wreath to form 4 equal center squares. Again, wire middle of 2 bundles and at either end for good support. Slip in extra branches as needed to strengthen squares.

5 Glue birds in place. They should sit firmly in middle bottom of each center square. Tilt birds forward so wreath still has a flat back. Glue small amounts of Spanish moss at base of each bird to resemble a nest.

6 Cut individual leaves and berries from holly. Glue into place around nest and to hide wire on wreath. Glue on roses. Glue pinecones between holly leaves and flowers.

7 Using small artist's paintbrush, brush tips of flowers, pinecones, and holly leaves lightly with glue. Sprinkle with diamond dust. If desired, sprinkle diamond dust on birds' feathers also. Let dry overnight.

Christmas Tree
Ornaments

*These ornaments are timeless and cute. Many will agree
that their inclusion on your tree is "on the button."*

what you'll need

Precut wood tree ornaments with hangers

Acrylic paint: gamel, forest green, spice brown, antique gold, white, and metallic gold

Brushes: #8 shader and 10/0 liner

Trims: assorted lengths of white and gold rickrack, material strips, red satin ribbon, gold trim, off-white rattail cord, cream sheer ribbon, ribbon roses, and gold cording

Scissors

Hot glue gun and glue sticks

Sparkle glaze

Assorted buttons

Precut ¾-inch wood star

Old toothbrush

Decorative snow

Floral accents: gold glitter spray and pale gold highlighter

Acrylic spray

*Clockwise from top: Victorian Bridal Tree; Country Tree; Traditional Gold Tree;
Child's Tree; Antique Memories Button Tree*

1 With shader brush, paint some ornaments gamel and some forest green. Paint tree trunks spice brown.

2 Child's Tree: Glue rickrack to tree; using shader brush paint with sparkle glaze. Let dry. Glue on pastel buttons. Tie a rickrack bow around hanger.

3 Country Tree: Using shader brush paint wood star antique gold. Tie a strip of material into a bow; glue to hanger. Glue star to tree. Glue burgundy and small white buttons to tree. Using liner brush and white paint, write "Noel" on trunk. Spatter-paint tree by dipping toothbrush into white paint and dragging finger across bristles. Let dry.

4 Antique Memories Button Tree: Tie a red satin bow, and glue to hanger. Glue on 4 old buttons, and spatter-paint tree with white paint. Dab snow with shader brush on tree and on tops of buttons. Let dry.

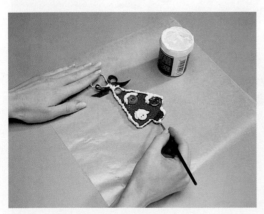

5 Victorian Bridal Tree: Glue gold trim and off-white rattail cord to tree. Tie bow of cream sheer ribbon to hanger. Glue ribbon rose to top of tree. Glue cream buttons to tree. Mist with gold glitter spray. Let dry.

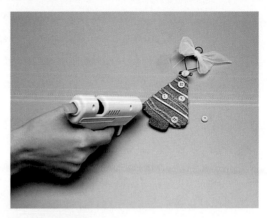

6 Traditional Gold Tree: Glue gold rickrack to tree. Tie bow of gold cording; glue to top of tree. Glue buttons to tree. Mist with gold highlighter. Let dry. Add dots using handle of liner brush dipped into metallic gold paint. Let dry.

7 Mist all trees with acrylic spray.

Holly
Table Runner

It's the small touches that can create the most beauty in a room. This quilted table runner is sure to be that spark in your yuletide decorating. And don't let the quilting intimidate you—with easy instructions and machine quilting, this table runner could be adorning your table with just a weekend of effort!

what you'll need

1½ yards muslin or neutral tone-on-tone fabric

¼ yard Christmas print for binding

¼ yard solid green fabric

½ yard solid red fabric

Iron and ironing board

Scissors

Yardstick

1½ yards fusible adhesive

Patterns on page 31

Sturdy paper or template material

Pencil

17×50-inch piece low-loft polyester batting

Straight pins

Large basting needle

Threads: ivory, green, and red

Zigzag sewing machine

See pages 5–6 for instructions on how to miter corners.

Size: 17×50 inches (after machine appliquéd and quilted)

1 Prewash and iron all fabrics. From muslin, cut two 17×50-inch pieces. From binding fabric, cut three 2×45-inch strips.

2 Cut two 9×17-inch pieces of fusible adhesive. Following manufacturer's directions, iron them side by side onto wrong side of green fabric. Make a template of holly leaf, and trace around it onto paper backing of green. Trace and cut out 66 holly leaves. Remove paper backing.

3 Cut two 18×17-inch pieces of fusible adhesive, and iron them side by side onto wrong side of red fabric. From template material, make full-size templates of remaining patterns. Trace around swag template 6 times onto paper backing of red fabric. Trace around bow template 8 times, and trace 33 holly berries. Cut out all motifs, and remove paper backing.

4 Center wreath guide on muslin, and lightly trace around it. The center point is 25 inches from each end and 8½ inches from each side.

Trace a circle with wreath guide on each end, 6½ inches from end and 4 inches from each side.

5 Place 11 holly leaves end to end on each wreath guide circle. End points of leaves should touch pencil line. Fuse.

6 Using photo as a guide, line up 11 more holly leaves on each wreath. Fuse 11 holly berries on each wreath between rows of holly leaves.

7 Evenly space swags around wreaths 1 inch from side edges of muslin. Fuse.

8 Center bows between and on ends of swags with bottom points 1 inch from muslin side edges. Fuse.

9 Sandwich batting between top and second piece of muslin, with right sides out. Pin along perimeter. With large needle and ivory thread, hand baste through all thicknesses vertically, horizontally, and around perimeter close to edge. Remove all pins.

10 Set sewing machine for a medium-width zigzag stitch, close enough for an outline satin stitch. Starting with green thread, stitch around edge of each holly leaf, quilting all layers together.

11 Change to red thread, and follow the same procedure to stitch holly berries, swags, and bows. When stitching is complete, remove all basting stitches except perimeter.

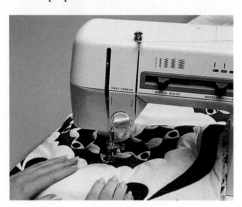

12 Stitch binding strips together to make a very long 2-inch strip. Fold strip in half lengthwise with wrong sides together. With raw edges even, stitch strip to top, joining binding ends. Miter corners. Turn binding to back, and hand- or machine-stitch into place.

Holly Berry

Bow

Wreath Guide

Swag

Holly Leaf

Enlarge each pattern 117%.

Pom
Reindeer Magnet

Kids can make these Pom Reindeer Magnets to hold their Christmas lists on the refrigerator. Before Santa comes, they can attach a note to the magnet that says, "Enjoy what's in the fridge!"

what you'll need

Poms: 1-inch beige, 2-inch brown, and ¼-inch red

White glue

Felt: 1×1-inch red and 2×2-inch brown

Scissors

Two wiggle eyes, 10mm each

Two beige chenille stems, 12 inches each

Ruler

Pattern on page 33

Tracing paper

Pencil

12-inch length of red rattail cord

Two gold jingle bells, 8mm each

¾-inch length of magnet strip, ½ inch wide

1 To make the head and the muzzle, glue the beige pom to the lower front part of the brown pom. For the nose, glue the red pom to the upper front part of the muzzle. Cut a smiling mouth shape from the red felt, and glue it below the nose. Glue the wiggle eyes to the head so that the bottom edges of the eyes touch the top of the muzzle.

2 Measure and cut one chenille stem into a 5-inch length and a 7-inch length. Measure and cut the other chenille stem into two 6-inch lengths; you will use only one of the 6-inch lengths, so set the other one aside. To make the antlers, line up the middles of the three lengths of chenille stem. Twist the stems in the middle to join them together. Arrange the stems so the 7-inch length is on the bottom, the 6-inch length is in between, and the 5-inch length is on top. Pinch and curl each of the six ends up to form the antlers, as in the drawing. Glue the middle of the antlers to the back of the head.

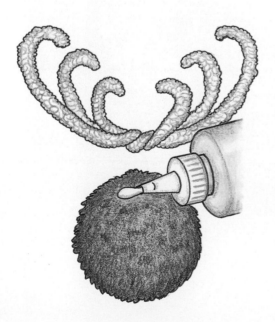

3 Using the pattern below, trace and cut two ears from the brown felt. Apply a dot of glue to the bottom of one ear; pinch the bottom together, and hold it for a moment. Repeat this gluing process to make the other ear. Glue the ears to the head just in front of the antlers.

4 Tie a bow in the rattail cord. Tie a jingle bell to each end of the rattail cord. Glue the bow beneath the muzzle. Glue the magnet strip to the back of the head.

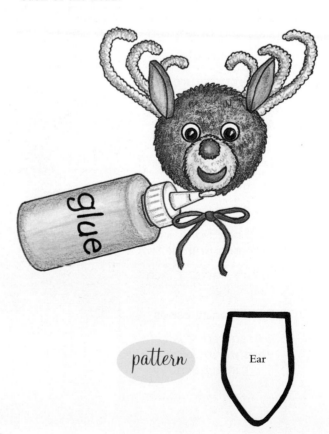

pattern   Ear

33

Fun in the
Forest

*These fun holiday decorations would make perfect gifts
for any of your friends. Apples, stars, or birds,
who could resist the whimsical appeal?*

what you'll need

Three 6-inch mini trees

Precut wood stars:
3-inch, 2-inch, and
36 assorted ¾- to
¼-inch lengths

Acrylic paint: gold,
cardinal red, dolphin
gray, and bright red

Paintbrush

Low-temperature glue
gun and glue sticks

3-inch wood apple
box set

Silver mini star garland

36 mini red apples

3- to 4-inch birdhouse

Small hand drill with
⅛-inch drill bit

8 bird's nests, 1 inch
each

Small candy canes

Assorted small
mushroom birds,
1 inch each

1 Star Tree: Basecoat all stars and base of 1 tree with gold. Apply second coat if needed. Let dry. Glue base of mini tree to 3-inch star.

2 Glue 2-inch star to treetop. Glue small stars to ends of branches. Larger stars should go toward bottom of tree.

3 Apple Tree: Paint apple box with cardinal red. Let dry.

4 Remove base of mini tree by twisting base until base pulls free, leaving only a thick wire at bottom. Apply glue into hole of apple box top, and insert tree wire. Let dry.

5 String mini star garland on tree starting at bottom and ending at top of tree. Glue mini red apples to ends of branches.

6 Bird Tree: Drill a hole at the top center of the birdhouse. Paint body of birdhouse gray. Paint roof, bottom, and perch with bright red. Let dry.

7 Remove base of mini tree by twisting base until base pulls free, leaving only a thick wire at bottom. Apply glue into hole at top of birdhouse, and insert tree wire. Let dry.

8 Glue bird's nests and candy canes to ends of branches. Glue mushroom birds to tips of other branches.

Great
Expectations

Select your favorite shade of wool for this elegant stocking, or make several out of different colors for the whole family!

what you'll need

200 yards heavy worsted weight 100% wool yarn (not superwash; this type of wool will not felt)

50 yards fuzzy 100% polyester yarn

U.S. size 10½ knitting needles

Ruler

Scissors

Tapestry needle

2 stitch holders

See pages 6–7 for knitting tips and abbreviations.

Gauge: 13 sts=4 inches in St st (before felting)
Size: 16 inches long (after felting)

1 Holding both yarns tog, CO 50 sts. P 1 row. Work in St st for 7 inches. End with k row. Cut fuzzy yarn, leaving 6-inch tail. Weave tail to WS with tapestry needle. Cont with wool yarn only. Work in St st for 11 more inches, measuring from last row with fuzzy yarn to row beneath needle. End with k row.

2 To make first ½ heel flap, p14; sl rem 36 sts onto a stitch holder. Turn and work in St st for additional 15 rows. End with k row. (Heel is turned using short rows, so some sts in row are not worked until later.)
Next row (Row 1): p3, p2tog, p1, turn (leave rem 8 sts on needle)
Row 2 and all RS rows: sl first st knitwise, k to end of row
Row 3: p4, p2tog, p1, turn
Row 5: p5, p2tog, p1, turn
Row 7: p6, p2tog, p1, turn
Row 9: p7, p2tog, p1, cut yarn
You will have 9 sts on needle. Sl them onto second stitch holder.

3 To make second ½ heel flap, start at other edge of stocking, and sl 14 sts purlwise from first stitch holder onto needle (leave center 22 sts on holder). With WS facing, rejoin yarn at 14th st, and p to end of row. Work in St st for additional 14 rows.

4 Next row (Row 1): k3, ssk, k1, turn (leave rem 8 sts on needle)
Row 2 and all WS rows: sl first st purlwise, p to end of row
Row 3: k4, ssk, k1, turn
Row 5: k5, ssk, k1, turn
Row 7: k6, ssk, k1, turn
Row 9: k7, ssk, k1 (do not turn) With 9 sts on needle, pick up 9 sts along side of heel flap. K across center 22 sts from holder, pick up 9 sts along side of first heel flap, and k rem 9 sts from holder (58 sts).

5 Row 1 and all odd number rows: p across all sts
Row 2: k17, k2tog, k20, ssk, k17
Row 4: k16, k2tog, k20, ssk, k16
Row 6: k15, k2tog, k20, ssk, k15
Row 8: k14, k2tog, k20, ssk, k14
Row 10: k13, k2tog, k20, ssk, k13 (48 sts). Work in St st for 5 inches. End with p row.

6 To make toe of stocking:
Row 1: [k6, k2tog] to end of row (42 sts)
Row 2 and WS rows: p across sts
Row 3: [k5, k2tog] to end of row (36 sts)
Row 5: [k4, k2tog] to end of row (30 sts)
Row 7: [k3, k2tog] to end of row (24 sts)
Row 9: [k2, k2tog] to end of row (18 sts)
Row 11: [k1, k2tog] to end of row (12 sts)
Row 13: [k2tog] to end of row (6 sts)

7 Cut yarn, leaving 18-inch tail. Thread end into tapestry needle, and draw needle through rem sts to close toe. Weave tail to WS. Fold stocking in half, and sew edges tog using simple overcast st. Cut more yarn and rethread needle as necessary. Fold cuff in half, and sew edge loosely to stocking working from the inside. Weave in all loose ends to WS and secure.

8 See page 6 for instructions on felting.

From Our Family
to Yours

Everyone loves receiving Christmas cards, especially when they are personal and handcrafted. With pictures of you and your family adorning the cards' covers, these lovely cards will be cherished and placed on display by your friends.

what you'll need

Blue art paper, cut into 10×7-inch rectangles (1 for each card)

Waxed paper

Snowflake rubber stamp

Silver pigment ink pad

Silver embossing powder

Embossing gun (or other heat source)

Extra-fine silver paint marker

Black photo corners (4 for each card)

3½×5-inch photograph (1 for each card)

1 Fold rectangles of blue paper to form 5×7-inch cards. Place card on sheet of waxed paper.

2 Apply silver ink to rubber stamp by brushing ink pad against surface of stamp.

3 Starting in a corner and working quickly but carefully, firmly press inked stamp to edge of card. Repeat around entire edge of card, reinking as necessary, to form a border of silver snowflakes. To make border look more natural, turn rubber stamp in different directions and allow some snowflakes to print off edge of card.

4 While ink is still wet, completely cover all stamped areas with embossing powder. Shake off excess powder, and return to bottle.

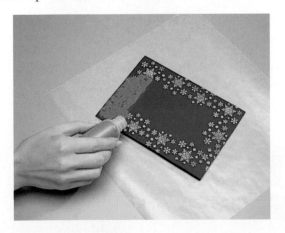

5 Using embossing gun, heat snowflakes until powder is melted and a shiny, raised surface is formed.

6 Use paint marker to write a holiday greeting inside of card.

7 Put photo corners on each corner of photograph. Moisten backs of photo corners, if necessary, and center photo on front of card, pressing down firmly.

Holiday Memories
Gone By

What a great way to reuse pretty cards! By covering this box with them, you're guaranteeing another reuse—of the box by the gift-getter.

what you'll need

Assorted Victorian holiday cards

Scissors

Sturdy box with separate top and bottom, approximately 10½×10½×2 inches

White glue

3 yards crimson moiré ribbon, 1⅜ inchES wide

Yardstick

1 Trim the holiday cards as desired. Glue the cards to the top of the box, overlapping as desired until the lid is completely covered. Let dry. (Extra glue may be required when folding cards around corners and sides of the box lid.) Repeat on the bottom of the box. Let dry.

2 To make the ribbon, place the covered box right side up. Cut ribbon into 1⅓-yard, 1-yard, and two ⅓-yard lengths. Using the 1⅓-yard length of ribbon, place the ribbon under the box with equal lengths extending. Bring the ends together at the center. Tie the ends into a single knot. Tie the 1-yard length into a bow over the first knot.

3 To make the double bow, form 2 loops with a ⅓-yard length, holding the loops securely in the center with thumb and forefinger.

4 Using the other ⅓-yard length, tie a bow around the center of the loops. With the ends, tie the second bow to the center of the first bow covering the knot. Trim the ends as desired.

wrapping options

Short on cards? First wrap the gift in red, green, or gold moiré. Instead of forming a card collage, randomly place a few Victorian or antique cards all over the package. Several coats of craft sealer applied to the top and bottom of the box will protect this unique gift. Be sure to allow the craft sealer to dry between coats.

Candy Cane
Serving Tray

What could be more fun and festive than a peppermint-designed serving tray? Matching hand-painted mugs filled with hot chocolate complete the holiday look.

what you'll need

11×14-inch wood serving tray with handles

8 wood toy wheels, 1¾ inches diameter

Sandpaper

Tack cloth

Acrylic paint: red and white

Paintbrushes: 1-inch foam and 2 small detail

Ruler

1-inch painter's tape

Craft knife

Pencil

Matte spray varnish

Hot glue gun and glue sticks

1 Lightly sand wood tray and toy wheels to remove any rough spots. Wipe with tack cloth to remove dust. Using foam brush, apply coat of red paint to entire tray and to toy wheels. Let dry. Lightly sand again, and wipe with tack cloth. Repeat painting, sanding, and tacking 2 more times. Let dry.

2 Starting about 1 inch from side of tray, apply strips of tape diagonally around 2 flat sides. Leave 1 inch between each strip. Allow tape to come over top edge and onto inside of tray. Make diagonal stripes along top edges of each handle, again leaving 1 inch between each tape strip. Trim ends of tape with craft knife, and press down tape edges to secure.

3 Using detail brush, paint with white between each strip of tape to create wide stripes. Let dry completely; remove tape.

4 To make smaller stripes within each 1-inch stripe, measure and mark ½ inch on first complete stripe. Affix tape diagonally along this mark, again wrapping tape over top edge and onto inside of tray (trim ends of tape on inside with craft knife).

5 Measure ¼ inch from edge of tape, and apply another piece of tape diagonally. Repeat across side of tray.

6 Repeat steps 4 and 5 on other flat side of tray.

7 Using detail brushes, paint between diagonal paint strips, using red paint on wide white stripes and white paint on wide red stripes. Let dry, and remove tape. Spray entire tray with 2 coats of matte varnish; let dry between coats.

8 Using detail brush, paint white stripe (1 inch at its widest point) on toy wheel. Make 2 more stripes, each 1 inch apart, to create a peppermint candy effect. Let dry. If desired, add ¼-inch stripes on wide stripes to match tray. Repeat for all wheels. Spray wheels with 2 coats of matte varnish; let dry between coats.

9 Stack 2 wheels together with a red stripe opposite a white stripe. Glue in place. Repeat with remaining wheels. Glue 1 stack of wheels to each corner of tray.

try this!

Embellish white ceramic mugs to go with your Candy Cane Serving Tray. Just use a red ceramic paint marker to add red stripes to the mug handles. Follow the manufacturer's instructions for care and handling.

Holly Jolly
Santas

Santa's jolly face will shine out at you from your own Christmas tree.
Spread some Christmas cheer by making one for each of your friends!

what you'll need

4-ounce package paper clay

Acrylic paint: beige, black, white, and blueberry

Resealable plastic bag

Stylus

Paintbrushes: #2 round and #12 flat

Spray mist bottle

Large paper clip

Wire cutters

White glue

3 yards sheer ivory wire-edged ribbon, ⅞ inch wide

Tape measure

Scissors

26-gauge silver wire

Pencil

4½ inches red wire-edged ribbon, 3 inches wide

Fabric glue

Small gold jingle bell

Cream blush

Acrylic sealer

1 Knead paper clay. Add 10 to 12 drops beige paint until color is well blended. Divide into 3 balls. While working with first ball, store other balls in plastic bag.

2 To create Santa's face, shape clay into an oval and flatten back side. Press tips of both fore-fingers into clay about ⅓ of the way down to create eye sockets. Pinch nose shape under eye sockets, and make nostrils in Santa's nose with tip of stylus. Poke eye openings with tip of paint-brush. (Mist clay occasionally to keep pliable; smooth out lines with fingertips.)

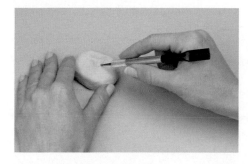

3 Use wire cutters to cut large U from paper clip. Bend ends of clip at 90-degree angle. Insert bent ends into back of head at top. Glue in place if necessary.

4 For beard, cut 9 to 10 pieces of ivory ribbon, each 8 inches long. Cut ends diagonally. Fold each piece in half over 2-inch lengths of wire. Twist wire tightly to pinch center of ribbon and secure. Wrap each ribbon end around pencil to

curl. Slide pencil out. Insert wire end into face. Arrange curls as desired.

5 For mustache, cut 2¼-inch length of ivory ribbon. Use wire to gather at center, and twist wire in place. At ends of ribbons, pinch ribbon wires together and tuck under to form mustache. Insert mustache beneath nose.

6 For hat, thread a 4-inch piece of wire length-wise through center of a 15-inch piece of ivory ribbon, creating a ruffle. Set aside. Turn under 1 cut edge of red ribbon, and glue. Let dry. Glue ruffle to right side of red ribbon along glued edge. Let dry. Gather other edge of red ribbon, and twist wire around it to secure gathers. Attach bell to gathered end of ribbon with wire. Turn wired edge under to back side of ribbon; pull ribbon wires out to cover edge. Glue to secure ribbon. Set aside.

7 Add eye details with #2 round paintbrush, unless noted otherwise. Paint eye opening black. Let dry. Paint eye opening with white, allowing an outline of black paint to show around the edge. Let dry. Paint iris with blueberry. Using stylus and black paint, dot pupil. Let dry. Add highlight dot of white paint in center of iris with smaller end of stylus. Add blush to cheeks with finger. When paint is dry, use #12 flat paintbrush to coat face with sealer. Let dry.

8 Glue hat in place. Shape hat as desired. Add ribbon to wire hanger if desired.

Candy-Coated
Christmas Wreath

You will see visions of sugarplums dancing in your head when you make this sparkling holiday wreath. Assorted miniature fruit, berries, and minty candy canes glisten with a "candy coating" of diamond dust.

what you'll need

54 pieces artificial fruit on wire picks

Small artist's paintbrush

White glue

Diamond dust or opalescent glitter

2 stems red berries

2 dozen plastic candy canes

Artificial pine wreath, 14 inches

Hot glue gun and glue sticks

1 With small artist's paintbrush, coat each piece of fruit with glue. Sprinkle diamond dust over fruit pieces. Repeat process on berries and candy canes. Let dry overnight.

2 Shape pine wreath by pulling out and fluffing branches.

3 Twist 3 pieces of different fruit together into a cluster. Place fruit clusters into wreath. Twist stems of fruit into branches. Continue around wreath until it is full.

4 Cut each berry stem into 5 or so pieces; each piece should have about 5 berries. Glue berry stems into wreath. Spread berries throughout wreath.

5 Glue candy canes into wreath at an angle so they stick out from fruits and berries.

Variation: For a variation, add a bow to this sparkling confection. Choose a soft color for the ribbon so you don't distract from the pastels of the fruit. Attach a small bow with streamers to the bottom of the wreath for an elegant look.

tip

When you store your wreath from year to year, some of the diamond dust might come off. You can easily touch up the wreath by brushing the pieces of fruit with a little more glue and adding a fresh sprinkling of diamond dust.

Snowflake Wrapping Paper

*The delicate pattern of snowflakes will generate
a blizzard of compliments! Like snowflakes and gift-getters,
this wrapping paper is one-of-a-kind.*

what you'll need

12 to 15 squares of paper, about 4½ square inches

Scissors

Iron and ironing board

White paper large enough for gifts

Plastic snowflakes (optional)

Blue spray paint

1 Fold bottom edge of square of paper up to top edge to make a rectangle. Fold this rectangle in half so you have a square. Fold this square from corner to corner to create a triangle.

2 With single fold at the bottom, fold down side with several creases to touch bottom edge. Cut off paper that hangs off end.

3 Cut out diamonds, circles, and odd shapes from multicreased side. Cut some designs on single-fold side, but don't cut it away completely. Unfold paper. Cut 12 to 15 snowflakes. With iron on coolest setting, press snowflakes so they lie flat. Iron sheets of white paper.

4 In a well-ventilated area, arrange snowflakes on white paper so they overlap slightly. If you have plastic snowflakes, use them to weigh down paper ones.

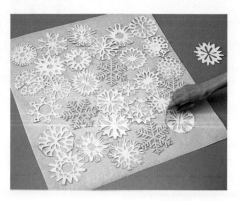

5 Shake can of paint well before spraying lightly over paper, using a gentle back-and-forth motion. Hold can high off paper, and spray directly above to avoid moving snowflakes. Allow to dry for a few minutes so you don't smudge paint when you remove snowflakes. Snowflakes can be reused.

Gingerbread Kid
Gift Tags

Who doesn't love presents? Gifts are even more enjoyable when they're decorated with cute gingerbread kids—they might just make your own children hunger for more.

what you'll need

Two 8¼×10¾-inch sheets opaque shrink plastic

Sandpaper

Patterns on page 51

Black medium-point permanent felt-tip marker

Pink and light brown acrylic paint

Paintbrush

Scissors

Hole punch

Ruler

Cookie sheet

Oven and oven mitts

34-inch length white baby rickrack

White glue

Four 7mm wiggle eyes

1 square inch green felt

Tracing paper

Pencil

Three ⅛-inch red buttons

2-inch length of 1-inch-wide green eyelet lace

6-inch length of ⅛-inch-wide red satin ribbon

16-inch length of red rattail cord

1 Read all instructions for shrinking plastic before beginning. Lightly sand both sheets of shrink plastic. Place each sheet on top of the gingerbread kid pattern below, and trace with a marker. Remove from the pattern. Paint pink circles for cheeks. Paint the rest with a thin coat of light brown; let dry. Cut out each shape. Punch a hole in each, ½ inch down from the top of the head. To shrink, follow manufacturer's instructions for baking on a cookie sheet; cool.

2 Cut two 14-inch lengths of rickrack. Attach one length around the edges of each shape, applying glue to the back of the rickrack a few inches at a time. Draw a smile and add a dot for the nose with the marker. Glue on the wiggle eyes, keeping them low for a cute look.

3 Using the pattern at right, trace and cut the tie from green felt. Glue the tie to the neck of one gift tag. Finish this one by gluing three red buttons down the front.

4 For the second gift tag, begin by gluing lace across the waist. Tie a bow in the ribbon, and glue it to the neck. For hair, cut and glue two 3-inch lengths of rickrack to the top of the head. Be careful not to cover the hole. Spot-glue hair at the sides of the head.

5 For the hanger loops, cut the rattail cord into two 8-inch lengths. Insert the end of one length through the hole on each gift tag. Using the two ends, tie a knot in each length.

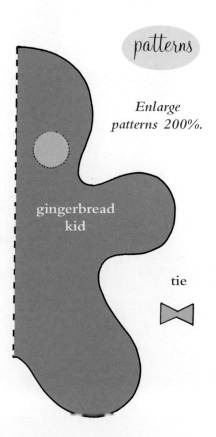

patterns

Enlarge patterns 200%.

gingerbread kid

tie

Bright Lights
Cookie Plate

Give your cookies that extra-special touch by presenting them on a plate decorated with hand-painted Christmas lights. Make your family's favorite treat to display on the plate!

what you'll need

Pattern on page 53

Scissors

Masking tape

Ruler

Clear, smooth 10-inch glass plate

Bottle-tip nozzle pen set

Enamel paint: black, green, white, yellow, red, and blue

Foam plate

#2 round paintbrushes

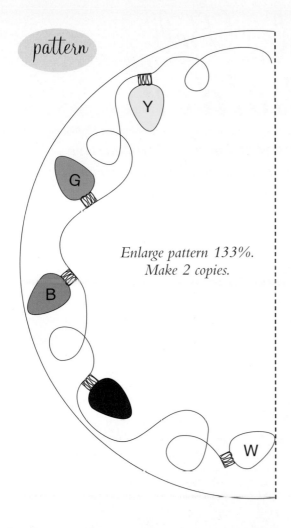

Enlarge pattern 133%.
Make 2 copies.

2 Using pen set, attach extension cap and fine metal tip to black enamel bottle. Practice squeezing lines of enamel from bottle onto foam plate, then draw thin black definition lines on glass plate for sockets and cords and around each bulb. Let dry. (Quickly and thoroughly rinse out cap and metal tip after each use.)

3 Thin small amount of green enamel with water on foam plate. Using pattern as your guide and painting on top of black definition lines, paint a line over coiling cord. Also use green to fill in sockets and 2 green bulbs. Be sure to apply paint strokes in same direction. Let dry, and repeat if necessary to achieve opaque coverage.

4 Thin small amount of white enamel with water, and paint white lightbulbs. Repeat with remaining paint colors to fill in yellow, red, and blue bulbs.

5 Follow manufacturer's instructions on enamel bottles for drying, baking, and curing enamel to glass.

1 Use copier to enlarge bulb pattern as indicated, and make 2 copies. Cut out patterns along semi-circle outline. Flip 1 pattern so ends of cord outline match up with other pattern, creating a continuous circular pattern. Tape in place. Snip ½-inch tabs all around pattern to allow paper to conform to plate. Position and tape pattern face-down on top of glass plate. Design will be painted on bottom of plate.

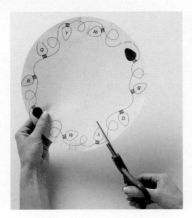

tip

Painting mistakes can be easily removed by washing them away with water before the paint has dried completely or by scraping the dried enamel off with your fingernail. Remember: Once the enamel has been cured, it becomes permanent.

Jolly Jingle Bell
Candleholder

Bring the spirit of holiday music into your home with this festive candleholder. Group a few together to create a wonderful centerpiece, or give one as a gift to your favorite holiday host.

what you'll need

9-inch-tall clear glass cylindrical vase with 3¼-inch opening

2×2 inches foam

Low-temperature glue gun and glue sticks

8 evergreen sprigs, 6 inches each

Scissors

3 sheet-music pages

1 yard gold metallic ribbon, 1¾ inches wide

Ruler

Floral wire

Wire cutters

2 red berry sprays, 12 inches each

6 holly leaves

48 gold jingle bells, assorted sizes

Clear glass votive holder

Red votive candle

1 Glue foam block to outside bottom of vase. This is where you will insert evergreens.

2 Place vase so foam block is on your right side. Insert and glue 2 evergreen sprigs horizontally at base of foam, one coming in front of foam and one extending away from foam. Cut remaining evergreens into short lengths, and fill in around already inserted evergreens.

3 Cut pages of sheet music in half horizontally. Tightly roll each section, and glue edges in place to secure. Cut 1 music roll in half, and insert and glue all rolled pages into evergreens.

4 About 6 inches from one end of gold ribbon, shape 2 loops about 3½ inches each. Pinch 2 loops together, and secure with short length of floral wire. Trim end of bow streamers to 4 inches, and cut V shape into end of each. Glue remaining ribbon trailing out back of design. Trim end of ribbon into V shape.

5 Cut 1 red berry spray in half, and insert a length vertically behind bow. Insert other section coming forward beneath bow. Cut other berry spray into short lengths, and insert around bow. Glue holly leaves into design around bow and music. Glue jingle bell to middle of bow; add more jingle bells as desired.

6 Fill vase with assorted jingle bells to about 3 inches from top. Place votive holder with candle inside vase.

Christmas Cowboy

Kids, grab your lassos because you'll want to catch this great Christmas craft idea. It's a cute Christmas Cowboy to tie up your time with fun.

what you'll need

7×7-inch piece of white cardboard

Scissors

White foam balls: one 3½-inch diameter, one 2½-inch diameter, and six 1-inch diameter

Low-temperature glue gun and glue sticks

Fiberfill

Patterns on page 57

Tracing paper

Pencil

Felt: 7×7-inch piece, red, and 1×1-inch piece, orange

Ruler

1-inch-wide yellow star sticker

Two wiggle eyes, 12mm each

6¼-inch length of red chenille stem

Two green poms, 1 inch each

4-inch brown felt cowboy hat

Small holly sprig

1-inch wreath

Two small wrapped gifts

Two ornaments, ½-inch each

1 For the base, trim the edges of the cardboard into an irregular curved shape. Slightly flatten one side of the large foam ball by pushing it firmly against the work surface. Glue the flat side of the ball to the center of the cardboard base. Slightly flatten one side of the medium foam ball, and then glue the flat side to the top of the large ball. Fluff up the fiberfill, and glue it to the base.

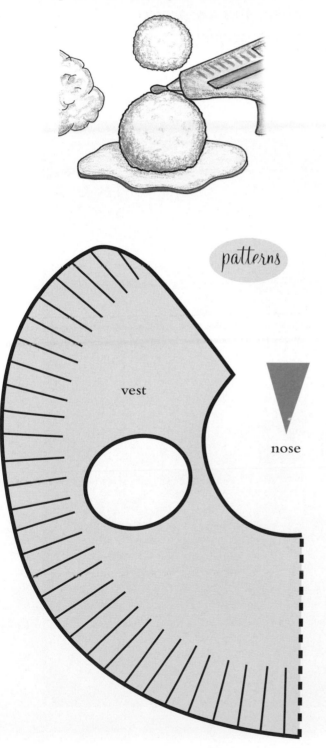

2 Using the pattern below, trace and cut out the vest from the red felt. Cut ½-inch slits around the bottom of the vest to create the fringe. Wrap the vest around the body of the snowman, and glue it in place. Attach the star sticker to the vest. To make the arm, glue three 1-inch foam balls to the side of the snowman, starting at the vest's arm-hole and moving down to the tummy. Repeat on the other side for the other arm.

3 Glue the wiggle eyes on the snowman's face. Using the pattern at left, trace and cut the nose from orange felt, and then glue it to the face. Cut a 1¼-inch piece of chenille stem, bend it into a smile, and then glue it to the face. Bend a ½-inch section at each end of the remaining 5-inch length of chenille stem. Insert one ½-inch end into the side of the snowman's head, curve the stem across the top of the head, and insert the other ½-inch end into the other side of the head. Glue the green poms over the ends of the stems.

patterns

vest

nose

4 Glue the hat to the top of the snowman's head. Glue the sprig of holly to the hatband. Glue the wreath in front of the snowman's hand, and glue the gifts and ornaments in the snow.

Pretty Present
Pins

What could be a better gift than a miniature version of, well, a gift? These pretty pins are perfect presents for all your favorite people!

what you'll need

Patterns on page 59

Shrink plastic

Pencil

Fine-tip permanent black felt pen

Permanent felt pens: red, white, and metallic gold

Scissors

Oven and oven mitts

Cookie sheet

Adhesive pin backing

White glue or low-temperature glue gun and glue sticks

1 Place a piece of shrink plastic over patterns at right, and trace them onto plastic with a pencil. Remove pattern, and retrace outline with black felt pen.

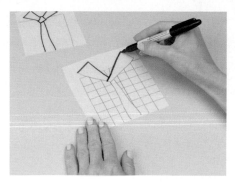

2 Color presents with colored felt pens. (Note: Do not use metallic gold until after plastic has been shrunk.)

3 Cut out presents. Follow manufacturer's instructions to heat shrink plastic on a cookie sheet in your oven.

4 When pieces have cooled, turn them over so the shiny side faces up. Add metallic gold. When dry, glue small present to large present.

5 Apply adhesive pin back to back of large present.

patterns

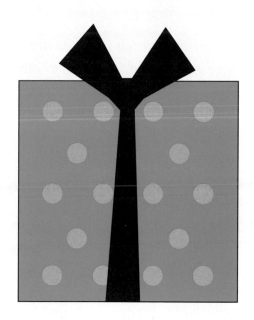

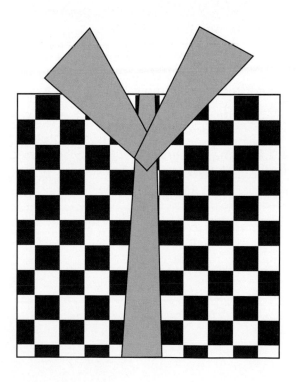

Holiday Cheer
Topiary

Add a touch of elegance to your Christmas-decorated home with a rosebud-studded topiary. An assortment of greens and long streamers of ribbon make it particularly eye-catching.

what you'll need

3- to 4-inch-diameter clay pot

Quick-drying floral spray paint: red and green

12-inch foam cone

⅓ block dry foam

Serrated knife

Low-temperature glue gun and glue sticks

6- to 7-inch twig

Handful Spanish moss

3 stems preserved springerii

4 stems preserved plumosus

2 stems dried boxwood

1 twig preserved cedar

2 to 3 stems preserved ming fern

Ruler

Floral knife (optional)

2 dozen dried red roses

2 to 3 stems dried red pepper berries

1 bunch dried red star flowers

Wood picks (optional)

3 yards red ribbon, ¼ inch wide

1 yard green ribbon, ⅜ inch wide

Florist wire

1 Spray clay pot red and foam cone green with quick-drying floral spray paint (or hobby paint). Allow to dry. Shape ⅓ block of foam to fit into clay pot (you may need to cut it with a serrated knife). Glue it in place. Insert and glue twig into base of foam cone, making sure it is centered. Insert and glue other end of twig into dry foam, leaving about a 3- to 4-inch tree trunk. Cover dry foam with Spanish moss.

2 Cut, if necessary, and evenly distribute 2- to 3-inch pieces of springerii, plumosus, boxwood, cedar, and ming fern over foam cone. Make sure to use smaller pieces at top and longer, fuller pieces at bottom.

3 Evenly distribute red roses over entire tree, using smaller pieces at top and longer, fuller pieces at bottom. Repeat with one or two red pepper berries and clusters of red star flowers. If stems are brittle, reinforce them with wood picks. To do so, place wired end of pick next to stem overlapping approximately ½ to 1 inch, and wind wire snugly around stem.

4 Make a bow from 2 yards of red ribbon (see page 9). Drape it over top of topiary to look like a garland. Make another bow from remaining 1 yard of red ribbon and 1 yard of green ribbon. Attach to base with florist wire. Insert a cluster of pepper berries next to ribbon.

Christmas
Partridge Tray

Serve your guests in style with this beautiful wooden tray with its holiday motif. Rich jewel-tone colors highlight this rendition of the familiar Christmas song.

what you'll need

Pattern on page 64

1 piece #11 white Aida cloth, 16×14 inches

6-strand cotton embroidery floss (see color key)

Embroidery scissors

Ruler

#24 tapestry needle

Embroidery hoop (optional)

12×9-inch rectangular tray (overall dimensions 16½×13 inches)

1 Locate center of design by lightly folding cloth in half and in half again to form quarters. Find center of chart by following arrows on sides. The center color of this pattern is black.

2 It may be easiest for you to start by stitching all of that color within center area, following chart (each square on chart equals one stitch on fabric). Begin by holding thread ends behind fabric until secured or covered over with two or three stitches (do not knot thread). Always cross all stitches in same direction. For horizontal rows, work stitches in two steps, i.e., all of left-to-right stitches and then all of right-to-left stitches.

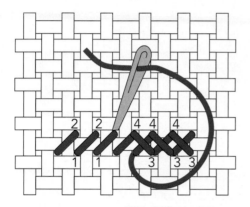

3 For vertical rows, work each complete stitch. You may skip a few stitches on back of material, but do not run thread from one area to another behind a section that will not be stitched in finished piece—it will show through fabric. If your thread begins to twist, drop needle and allow thread to untwist. It is important to final appearance of project to keep an even tension when pulling stitches through so that all stitches will have a uniform look.

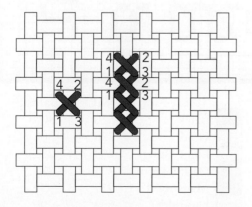

4 To end a thread, weave or run thread under several stitches on back side. Cut ends close to fabric.

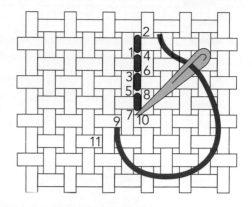

5 Continue with piece by selecting other colors and stitching all of that color within an area. Backstitch to create letters and to finish stitching. If you are using an embroidery hoop, you may want to remove it when you're not working.

6 Fill in unmarked areas inside black border with aqua. Mount in tray using manufacturer's directions. (To preserve finished piece, you may want to place a piece of glass over design; tray can also be framed as a wall picture.)

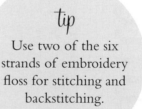

tip

Use two of the six strands of embroidery floss for stitching and backstitching.

		DMC	Bates
	Black	310	403
	Gold	725	306
	Light Green	704	255
	Dark Green	701	227
	Magenta	917	89
	Lavender	554	90
	Purple	552	101
	Aqua	807	168

pattern